LOTS OF LIMERICKS

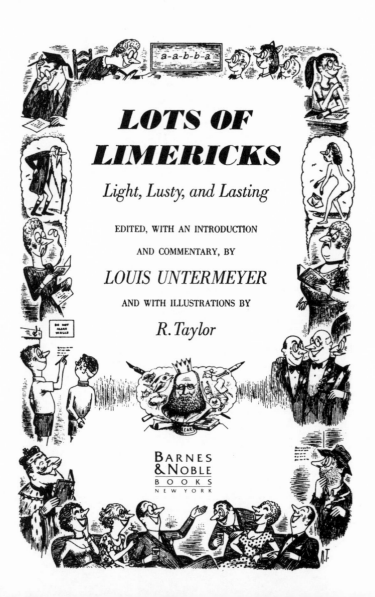

LOTS OF LIMERICKS

Light, Lusty, and Lasting

EDITED, WITH AN INTRODUCTION

AND COMMENTARY, BY

LOUIS UNTERMEYER

AND WITH ILLUSTRATIONS BY

R. Taylor

BARNES
&NOBLE
BOOKS
NEW YORK

Copyright © 1961 by Louis Untermeyer
Illustrations © 1961 by Richard Taylor
All rights reserved.

This edition published by Barnes & Noble, Inc., by
arrangement with the Estate of Louis Untermeyer, Norma
Anchin Untermeyer c/o Professional Publishing Services. This
edition was reprinted with expressed permission by Laurence S.
Untermeyer and the Estate of Richard Taylor.

1994 Barnes & Noble Books

ISBN 1-56619-375-3

Printed and bound in the United States of America

M 9 8 7 6 5 4 3 2

Acknowledgments

The publisher and editor have made every effort to trace the ownership of all copyrighted material contained in this volume. In the event of any question arising as to any use of the material, they, while expressing regret for any error unconsciously made, will be pleased to make the necessary correction in future editions of this volume.

The adaptations in the last two sections are by the editor.

Contents

Introduction: The Limerick, Its Life and High Times

In 1953 there appeared a thick volume with the non-committal title *The Limerick*. Published in Paris over the deceptively academic imprint of *Les Hautes Études*, it contained 1700 unacademic examples of the familiar form with variants. It mentioned some twenty-seven previous torrid compilations (mostly unpublished), and the contents were arranged under such headings (to name the more printable ones) as "Little Romances," "Organs," "Strange Intercourse," "Virginity," "Prostitution," "Sex Substitutes," "Assorted Eccentricities," "Weak Sisters," and "Chamber of Horrors." Obviously the book could not be circulated through the U.S. mail, but its graphic (or pornographic) contents showed how far and how shamelessly the simple, little five-line stanza had gone.

The career of the limerick has been a curious one. It started in all innocence. The place of origin is uncertain, although some scholars claim it is of Irish descent. This theory is based on scanty evidence, little more than an Irish song, each verse of which ends, "We'll all come up, come up to Limerick." Long before the limerick acquired fame—or even its name—it was appearing sporadically in books for children under the aegis of Mother Goose. Among other nursery rhymes there can be found so exemplary a stanza as:

There was an old lady of Leeds
Who spent all her time in good deeds;
    She worked for the poor
    Till her fingers were sore,
This pious old lady of Leeds.

These lines occurred in what is now conceded to be the first book devoted to limericks (although the word itself was not used), *The History of Six-teen Wonderful Old Women,* published in 1821. It was followed a year or two later by *Anecdotes and Adventures of Fifteen Gentlemen,* one of which was much quoted:

There was a sick man of Tobago
Lived long on rice-gruel and sago;
    But at last, to his bliss,
    The physician said this:
"To a roast leg of mutton you *may* go."

The oddity of the idea as well as the oddity of the verse form caught the fancy of Edward Lear who, as we shall see in the section entitled "The Old Classics," popularized the limerick, although he, too, never employed the term.

If the origin of the word remained in obscurity, the form did not. It became the favorite of people everywhere, from serious poets to naughty schoolboys, from housewives trying to supply the fifth line in a contest which would win them an automatic dish-washer to their husbands rowdily regaling their companions at a stag party. Before it was varied by specialists, the formula was childishly simple. It consisted of five lines which almost inevitably began: "There was a young lady of . . ." or "There was an old man from . . ."

For the most part, the formula is still maintained. The five lines are always built on no more (and no less) than two rhymes (the rhymes being expressed by the symbol a-a-b-b-a), with the third and fourth lines one foot shorter than the other three. Now and then some foolhardy experimenter attempts to extend the limerick by altering the shape, adding an extra line. But all such changes destroy the character and compactness of the pure form. To the aficionado, there cannot be a six-line limerick any more than there can be a fifteen-line sonnet. As far as form is concerned, the following, one of Mother Goose's jingles, is a quite perfect limerick, and probably the most ancient:

Hickory, dickory, dock!
The mouse ran up the clock.
 The clock struck one—
 The mouse ran down.
Hickory, dickory, dock!

After Lear, the limerick grew fantastically. It embraced every topic, territory, and temperament; nothing was too sacred or too obscene for those five small lines. The limerick absorbed solemnities and absurdities, traditional legends and off-color jokes, devout reflections and downright indecencies without a quiver or the loss of a syllable. It refused to recognize borderlines or any other limits.

One indication of its geographical range is a collection, 99 *Limericks*, published recently by a firm in Munich. Although the limericks themselves are printed in English, the German translations and learned commentaries are in Germanic prose. They demonstrate that, although its basic appeal is international, the limerick loses its quality and its point becomes pointless when it has to be filtered through another language.

A perfectly innocuous limerick illustrates the language problem:

There was a young fellow named Hall
Who fell in the spring in the fall.
'Twould have been a sad thing
Had he died in the spring.
But he didn't—he died in the fall.

The pun about dying in the spring instead of the fall completely stymied the translator. Thereupon he resorted to *two* translations. In one the word "spring" was given as *Frühjahr* (the season), in the other it became *Quelle* (a flow of water), while "fall" was rendered both as *Herbst* (the season) and *Wasserfall* (waterfall).

For a while it looked as if the limerick would be at home only in its mother country; it seemed as

English as cricket, Big Ben, afternoon tea and crumpets. But it attained strange growths while keeping its character—or losing it. Countless collections, ranging from the polite to the unspeakable, from fun to filth, were mimeographed and secretly circulated. It surprised many to learn that Norman Douglas, author of the delicately stylized *South Wind,* was also the author of the scatological *Some Limericks,* and that Arnold Bennett, John Galsworthy, Rudyard Kipling, and T. S. Eliot were devotees of the racier specimens of the form.

This collection has a broader range than most. It includes traditional as well as modern examples, a generous sampling of the best English models and the most recent American innovations. It does not disdain to reprint the wildly nonsensical and, though it does not print the merely obscene or baldly indecent, it offers interesting adaptations of the hitherto unprintable.

Faced with thousands of all sorts of limericks, the editor's test has been this: Are they clever? Are they well-made? Are they wittily turned? Are they frankly funny? Every inclusion in the following pages passes one or more of these tests. The best of them fulfill all the requirements of the true lover of limericks. They may even convince a few sheltered souls who persist in hating them.

L.U.

LOTS OF LIMERICKS

THE OLD CLASSICS

If Geoffrey Chaucer is the father of English poetry, Edward Lear is unquestionably the father of the limerick. Lear did not invent the form, but he was the first to bring it into favor and international fame. This accomplishment was the thing of which he was least proud, for rhyming was merely one of Lear's casual pastimes. A serious artist, his paintings of birds were often compared to Audubon's. Lear was an expert water-colorist. He gave drawing lessons to Queen Victoria, and his topographical designs were so accurate that experts recognized the geology of a country from Lear's sketches.

Because of his reputation Lear was engaged by the Earl of Derby to paint his private menagerie; in his spare time he entertained the Earl's children with nonsense verses made of moonshine and magic. It was during this period that Lear discovered the limerick. Reading "There was a sick man of Tobago" (quoted on p. 11) he felt, as he wrote many years later, that it was "a form of verse lending itself to limitless variety for rhymes and pictures; and thenceforth the greater part of the original drawings and verses for the first *Book of Nonsense* were struck off."

In spite of the possibilities which Lear saw in the "limitless variety for rhymes," he scarcely took advantage of them. Part of the charm of the limerick is the surprise, the sudden swoop and unexpected twist of the last line. With few exceptions, Lear ignored the whiplash ending which makes the modern limerick so effective. He rarely introduced a new rhyme at the conclusion; practically all his last lines are repetitions or slight variations of the first line.

Nevertheless, Lear's limericks set the pattern for a long time. He revelled not only in peculiar rhymes but in warm good humor, wild whimsicality, and carefree nonsense. His absurdities are still delightful and sometimes uproarious; his "plots" are breathtaking; his adjectives are strange but logical, his fantasies inexhaustible. The spell which they evoke is still potent.

Here are fifteen of Lear's limericks—he himself composed more than two hundred of them—all with his characteristic "Queery Leary" laughable and inimitable touch.

There was an old man of Cape Horn
Who wished he had never been born;
　　So he sat on a chair
　　Till he died of despair
That dolorous man of Cape Horn.

There was a young lady of Greenwich
Whose garments were bordered with spinach;
　　But a large spotty calf
　　Bit her shawl quite in half,
Which alarmed that young lady of Greenwich.

There was an old person of Cromer
Who stood on one leg to read Homer.
　　When he found he grew stiff
　　He jumped over the cliff,
Which concluded that person of Cromer.

There was a young lady of Norway,
Who casually sat in a doorway.
>   When the door squeezed her flat,
>   She exclaimed, "What of that!"
This courageous young lady of Norway.

There was a young lady in blue,
Who said, "Is it you? Is it you?"
>   When they said, "Yes, it is,"
>   She replied only "Whizz!"
That ungracious young lady in blue.

There was an old man who said, "Hush!
I perceive a young bird in the bush."
>   When they said, "Is it small?"
>   He replied, "Not at all.
It is four times as big as the bush!"

There was an old man who supposed
That the street door was partially closed;
    But some very large rats
    Ate his coats and his hats,
While that futile old gentleman dozed.

There was an old man, who when little
Fell casually into a kettle;
    But, growing too stout
    He could never get out,
So he passed all his life in that kettle.

There was an old person of Anerly,
Whose conduct was strange and unmannerly;
    He rushed down the strand
    With a pig in each hand,
But returned in the evening to Anerly.

There was an old person of Ware
Who rode on the back of a bear;
　　When they said, "Does it trot?"
　　He said: "Certainly not,
It's a Moppsikon Floppsikon bear."

There was an old person of Wick,
Who said, "Tick-a-Tick, Tick-a-Tick,
　　Chickabee, Chickabaw,"
　　And he said nothing more,
This laconic old person of Wick.

There was an old person of Woking,
Whose mind was perverse and provoking;
　　He sat on a rail,
　　With his head in a pail,
That illusive old person of Woking.

There was an old man with a beard,
Who said, "It is just as I feared.
    Two owls and a hen,
    Four larks and a wren,
Have *all* built their nests in my beard!"

There was an old man of Thermopylae,
Who never did anything properly;
    But they said: "If you choose
    To boil eggs in your shoes,
You cannot remain in Thermopylae."

There was a young lady whose chin
Resembled the point of a pin:
    So she had it made sharp
    And purchased a harp,
And played several tunes with her chin.

Toward the end of the nineteenth century the limerick was accepted not only as a laugh-provoker but as an established verse form. Famous versifiers and even poets tried their hand at producing variations on the old model. Lear had written a limerick about a man who was, in both senses, bored by a bee. It ran:

There was an old man in a tree,
Who was horribly bored by a bee.
When they said, "Does it buzz?"
He replied, "Yes, it does!
It's a regular brute of a bee."

In one of his more mischievous moments,
W. S. Gilbert (this time without the aid of Sullivan)
burlesqued Lear's lines. Gilbert, who rollicked in
rhyme and outrhymed any poet of his day, wrote a
limerick that had no rhymes at all:

There was an old man of St. Bees.
Who was stung in the arm by a Wasp.
When asked, "Does it hurt?"
He replied, "No, it doesn't;
I'm *so* glad that it wasn't a Hornet."

Lewis Carroll, Lear's compeer in the kingdom
of nonsense, offered the following:

There was a young man of Oporta,
Who daily got shorter and shorter.
    The reason he said
    Was the hod on his head,
Which was filled with the heaviest mortar.

Oliver Wendell Holmes found the limerick to his liking. He was not, as the phrase goes, an irresponsible punster. On the contrary, he was a highly responsible author and relished the pun for its incisiveness, even though he ruined a medical career when, waiting for patients, he said he would be grateful for small fevers. His punning limerick is one of the most quoted and also one of the finest of its kind.

The Reverend Henry Ward Beecher
Called a hen a most elegant creature.
    The hen, pleased with that,
    Laid an egg in his hat—
And thus did the hen reward Beecher.

Robert Louis Stevenson extended the geographical range—limericks usually insisted on taking place in a particularly odd region. Stevenson supplied this childishly convincing stanza, which is not to be found in *A Child's Garden of Verses:*

There was an old man of the Cape
Who made himself garments of crêpe.
    When asked, "Do they tear?"
    He replied, "Here and there;
But they're perfectly splendid for shape."

Rudyard Kipling was another who succumbed to the quick charm of the limerick. In it he showed a grotesque humor rarely found in his more serious work. For example:

There once was a boy in Quebec,
Who was buried in snow to his neck.
    When asked, "Are you friz?"
    He replied, "Yes, I is.
But we don't call this cold in Quebec."

Gelett Burgess, the humorist who added to the language such words as "blurb" and "bromide" (meaning an outworn platitude) is remembered as the man who wrote "I never saw a purple cow." But Burgess was equally himself in such limericks as:

I wish that my room had a floor;
I don't care so much for a door;
But this walking around
Without touching the ground
Is getting to be quite a bore.

I'd rather have fingers than toes;
I'd rather have ears than a nose;
And as for my hair,
I'm glad it's still there.
I'll be awfully sad when it goes.

Eugene Field was one of the first to see the humorous possibilities in the difference between

spelling and pronunciation. Following a kind of ty-
pographical logic, he came up with this:

Now what in the world shall we dioux
With the bloody and murderous Sioux,
    Who some time ago
    Took an arrow and bow
And raised such a hellabelioux?

By the beginning of the twentieth century the
trade in limericks was flourishing. Often frowned on
in public, they were practiced everywhere in private.
Most of them died the quick death of ephemeral
things, but many survived to attain a lasting popu-
larity. Here are some of the limericks which have
attained such eminence that they might well be
classified as The Old Classics. The first and inciden-
tally, best known, has been continually quoted as
the work of that most prevalent of authors: Anony-
mous. It is, however, the brain-child of a witty
Englishman, Cosmo Monkhouse.

There was a young lady of Niger,
Who smiled as she rode on a tiger.
They returned from the ride
With the lady inside—
And the smile on the face of the tiger!

A diner while dining at Crewe
Found a rather large mouse in his stew.
Said the waiter, "Don't shout
And wave it about,
Or the rest will be wanting one, too."

There was an old man from Nantucket
Who kept all his cash in a bucket.
    His daughter, named Nan,
    Ran away with a man
And as for the bucket, Nantucket.

The Nantucket limerick bred many imitations. Columnists, casual contributors, and college magazines competed to supply sequels. The following is perhaps the best of the series.

He followed the pair to Pawtucket—
The man and the girl with the bucket—
    And he said to the man
    He was welcome to Nan,
But as for the bucket, Pawtucket.

There was a young fellow from Clyde
Who was once at a funeral spied.

When asked who was dead,
    He smilingly said,
"I don't know. I just came for the ride."

There was a composer named Liszt
Whose music no one could resiszt.
    When *he* swept the keyboard
    Nobody could *be* bored;
And now that he's gone he is miszd.

A glutton who came from the Rhine
When asked at what hour he would dine,
    Replied, "At eleven,
    At three, five, and seven,
And eight and a quarter past nine."

There was a young man from Laconia
Whose mother-in-law had pneumonia
    He hoped for the worst,
    And after March first,
They buried her 'neath a begonia.

There was a young joker named Tarr,
Who playfully pickled his ma.
When he finished his work
He remarked with a smirk,
"This will make quite a family jar."

A reckless young man from Fort Blaney
Made love to a spinster named Janie.
When his friends said, "Oh dear,
She's so old and so queer."
He replied, "But the day was *so* rainy!"

There was a young lady from Rye
With a shape like a capital I.
When they said, "It's too bad,"
She learned how to pad.
Which shows you that figures can lie.

There once was a boy of Bagdad,
An inquisitive sort of a lad.
    He said, "Let us see
    If a sting has a bee."
And he very soon found out it had.

There was an old lady of Wales
Who lived upon oysters and snails.
    Upon growing a shell,
    She exclaimed, "It is well.
Now I'll never wear bonnets or veils."

There was a young woman of Glasgow,
Whose party proved quite a fiasco;
   At nine-thirty, about,
   The lights all went out
Through a lapse on the part of the Gas Co.

There was a young person from Perth
Who was born on the day of his birth.
   He was married, they say,
   On his wife's wedding day,
And died when he quitted this earth.

41

There once was a spinster from Wheeling
Endowed with such delicate feeling
    That she thought any chair
    Should not have its legs bare,
So she kept her eyes fixed on the ceiling.

There's a clever old miser who tries
Every method to e-con-omize.
    He said with a wink,
    "I save gallons of ink
By simply not dotting my i's."

Said the fair-haired Rebecca of Klondike,
"Of you I'm exceedingly fond, Ike.
    To prove I adore you
    I'll dye, darling, for you,
And be a brunette, not a blonde, Ike."

There was an old maid of Vancouver,
Who captured a man by maneuver.
    She jumped on his knee
    With some rare *eau de vie*,
And nothing on earth could remove her.

A railroad official at Crewe
Met an engine one day that he knew.
     Though he nodded and bowed,
     The engine was proud,
And cut him—it cut him in two.

There was an old man of Tarentum,
Who gnashed his false teeth till he bent 'em.
     When they asked him the cost
     Of what he had lost,
He replied, "I can't say; I just rent 'em."

There was a young lady of Venice,
Who used hard-boiled eggs to play tennis.
 When they said, "It seems wrong."
 She remarked, "Go along!
You don't *know* how prolific my hen is!"

There was a brave damsel from Brighton,
Whom nothing could possibly frighten.
 She plunged in the sea
 And with infinite glee
Rode away on the back of a Triton.

There was a young man of South Bay,
Making fireworks one summer day.
    He dropped his cigar
    In the gunpowder jar . . .
There *was* a young man of South Bay.

There was a young girl, a sweet lamb,
Who smiled as she entered a tram.
    After she had embarked
    The conductor remarked,
"Your fare." And she said, "Yes, I am."

A new servant maid named Maria,
Had trouble in lighting the fire.
 The wood being green,
 She used gasoline . . .
Her position by now is much higher!

A tone-deaf old person from Tring
When somebody asked him to sing,
 Replied, "It is odd
 But I cannot tell *God*
Save the Weasel from *Pop Goes the King.*"

"I must leave here," said Lady de Vere,
"For these damp airs don't suit me, I fear."
 Said her friend, "Goodness me!
 If they do not agree
With your system, why eat pears, my dear?"

A sensitive girl named O'Neill
Once went up in the big Ferris Wheel;
    But when half-way around
    She looked down at the ground,
And it cost her a two-dollar meal.

A housewife called out with a frown
When surprised by some callers from town,
    "In a minute or less
    I'll slip on a dress"—
But she slipped on the stairs and came down.

There was a young lady of Kent,
Who always said just what she meant;
      People said, "She's a dear—
      So unique—so sincere—"
But they shunned her by common consent.

There was a young fellow from Tyne
Put his head on the South-Eastern Line;
      But he died of ennui,
      For the 5:53
Didn't come till a quarter past nine.

There was a young lady of Crete,
Who was so exceedingly neat,
      When she got out of bed
      She stood on her head,
To make sure of not soiling her feet.

There was a faith-healer of Deal,
Who said, "Although pain isn't real,
    If I sit on a pin,
    And it punctures my skin,
I dislike what I fancy I feel."

There once was a pious young priest,
Who lived almost wholly on yeast;
    "For," he said, "it is plain
    We must all rise again,
And I want to get started at least."

There was a young man who was bitten
By twenty-two cats and a kitten.
    Cried he, "It is clear
    My end is quite near.
No matter! I'll die like a Briton!"

There was a dear lady of Eden,
Who on apples was quite fond of feedin';
    She gave one to Adam,
    Who said, "Thank you, Madam,"
And then both skedaddled from Eden.

There once was a girl of New York
Whose body was lighter than cork;
    She had to be fed
    For six weeks upon lead,
Before she went out for a walk.

There was an old man who said, "Do
Tell me how I'm to add two and two.
    I'm not very sure
    That it doesn't make four—
But I fear that is almost too few."

A Turk named Abdullah Ben Barum
Had sixty-five wives in his harem.
    When his favorite horse died,
    "Mighty Allah," he cried,
"Take a few of my wives. I can spare 'em."

The poor benighted Hindoo,
He does the best he kindo.
   He sticks to caste
   From first to last.
For pants he makes his skindo.

The appeal of the little stanza became so widespread that when people could not make up limericks, they appropriated them. Woodrow Wilson was so fond of a particularly modest limerick, "The Face," that he was later credited with its authorship; it appeared in almost every anthology over his name. It was, however, the work of a minor poet, Anthony Euwer, and it was part of a sequence called "Limeratomy," a word which, explained Euwer, combined "limerick" and "anatomy." The following trio are from that sequence.

THE HANDS

The hands, they were made to assist
In supplying the features with grist.
    There are only a few—
    As a rule about two—
And are hitched to the end of the wrist.

THE FACE

As a beauty I'm not a great star,
There are others more handsome by far,
    But my face, I don't mind it,
    Because I'm behind it—
'Tis the folks in the front that I jar.

THE SMILE

No matter how grouchy you're feeling,
You'll find the smile more or less healing.
    It grows in a wreath
    All around the front teeth—
Thus preserving the face from congealing.

A SAMPLER OF CURRENT FAVORITES

As we have seen in the preceding section, later practitioners of the art enjoyed Lear's fantasies, but they felt he was somewhat limited. They found the repetition of the same rhyming word monotonous and unnecessary. They gave the old form new turns and twists; they came up with surprises, unpredictable rhymes, and astonishing non sequiturs.

Still greater changes were apparent in twentieth century limericks. Besides the improvement in technique, the tone became freer. In spite of the abbreviated size of the limerick, the area was somehow extended. Writers of light verse and lyrical poets, essayists, anthologists, and novelists were among those who turned out limericks with deftness and despatch.

This section of current favorites shows temperamental as well as technical advances on Lear's guile-

less limericks. A distinctive sampler, it starts off
properly enough with distinguished names.

There was a young man of Montrose
Who had pockets in none of his clothes.
    When asked by his lass
    Where he carried his brass,
He said, "Darling, I pay through the nose."

ARNOLD BENNETT

It's time to make love. Douse the glim.
The fireflies flicker and dim.
    The stars lean together
    Like birds of a feather,
And the loin lies down with the limb.

CONRAD AIKEN[1]

---

[1] Aiken, poet, novelist, and Pulitzer Prize winner, has given this
verse an appropriate and punning title. He calls it "Limberick."
Copyright, 1956, by Louis Untermeyer.

An angry young husband named Bickett
Said, "Turn yourself round and I'll kick it.
    You have painted my wife
    In the nude to the life.
Do you think, Mr. Greene, that was cricket?"

JOHN GALSWORTHY

There was a young lady named Choate,
Whose pleasure it was to emote.
    She would say with a tear,
    "I am not wanted here!"
Then get up and take off her coat.

WILLIAM JAY SMITH[2]

Ogden Nash and Morris Bishop are America's most brilliant versifiers; they have given light verse new measure and critical meaning. Both have experimented widely in subject matter and structure, not neglecting the limerick.

There was an old miser named Clarence
Who simonized both of his parents.
    "The initial expense,"
    He remarked, "Is immense,
But I'll save it in wearance and tearance."

OGDEN NASH[3]

[2] Hitherto unpublished, and copyrighted as a part of this book.

[3] From *The Face Is Familiar* by Ogden Nash. Copyright, 1940, by Ogden Nash. Used by permission of Little, Brown & Company, Curtis Brown Ltd., and J. M. Dent & Sons Ltd.

There was a young belle of old Natchez
Whose garments were always in patchez.

When comment arose

On the state of her clothes,

She drawled, "When Ah itchez, Ah scratchez."

OGDEN NASH[4]

[4] From *The Face Is Familiar* by Ogden Nash. Copyright, 1938, by Ogden Nash. Used by permission of Little, Brown & Company, and Curtis Brown Ltd.

Said old Peeping Tom of Fort Lee:
"Peeping ain't what it's cracked up to be;
    I lose all my sleep,
    And I peep and I peep . . .
And I find 'em all peeping at *me!*"

MORRIS BISHOP[5]

There's a tiresome young man in Bay Shore;
When his fiancée cried, "I adore
    The beautiful sea!"
    He replied, "I agree
It's pretty. But what is it *for?*"

MORRIS BISHOP[5]

Said a fervent young lady of Hammels,
"I object to humanity's trammels!
    I want to be free!
    Like a bird! Like a bee!
Oh, why am I classed with the mammals!"

MORRIS BISHOP[5]

[5] From *Spilt Milk* by Morris Bishop. Copyright, 1942, by Morris Bishop. Reprinted by permission of G. P. Putnam's Sons.

The rest of this section begins with a limerick which has been constantly collected, misquoted and rarely credited to anyone. Its author is Langford Reed, an English wit, poet, and compiler.

An indolent vicar of Bray
His roses allowed to decay.
    His wife, more alert,
    Bought a powerful squirt
And said to her spouse, "Let us spray."

I sat next to the Duchess at tea,
Distressed as a person could be.
    Her rumblings abdominal
    Were simply phenomenal—
And everyone thought it was me!

There were once two young people of taste
Who were beautiful down to the waist.
    So they limited love
    To the regions above,
And thus remained perfectly chaste.

An unfortunate dumb mute from Kew
Was trying out signs that were new.
    He did them so fast
    That his fingers at last
Got tangled and fractured a few.

There was a young lass from Dundee
Whose knowledge of French was "Oui, oui."
    When they asked, "Parlez vous?"
    She replied, "Same to you."
A fine bit of fast repartee.

There was an old lady who said
When she found a thief under her bed,
    "Get up from the floor;
    You're too near the door,
And you may catch a cold in your head."

There was a young man of high station
Who was found by a pious relation
    Making love in a ditch
    To—I won't say a bitch—
But a woman of *no* reputation!

There was a young fellow named Hyde,
Who fell through an outhouse and died.
    His unfortunate brother,
    He fell through another;
And now they're interred side by side.

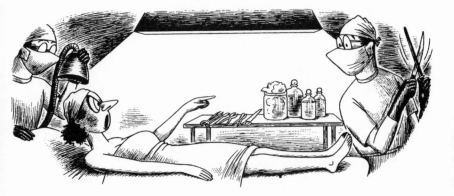

A girl being treated for hernia
Remarked to her doctor, "Goldernia,
    When slicing my middle,
    Be sure not to fiddle
With matters that do not concernya."

A pious old Jew from Salonika
Said "For Christmas I'd like a harmonica."
    His wife, to annoy him,
    Said, "Feh! That's for *goyim!*"
And gave him a jews-harp for Chanukah.

To his wife said a grumbler named Dutton,
"I'm a gourmet, I am, not a glutton.
    For ham, jam, or lamb
    I don't give a damn.
Come on, let's return to our mutton."

Said a foolish householder of Wales,
"An odor of coal-gas prevails,"
    She then struck a light,
    And later that night
Was collected in seventeen pails.

There was a young man at the War Office,
Whose brain was no good as a store office.
    Every warning severe
    Simply went in one ear
And out at the opposite orifice.

There was a good Canon of Durham
Who fished with a hook and a worrum.
    Said the Dean to the Bishop,
    "I've brought a big fish up,
But I fear we will have to inter'm."

A young schizophrenic named Struther
When told of the death of his mother,
    Said, "Yes, it's too bad,
    But I can't feel too sad.
After all, I *still* have each other."

A collegiate damsel named Breeze,
Weighed down by B.A.'s and Litt. D.'s,
    Collapsed from the strain.
    Alas, it was plain
She was killing herself by degrees.

There once was a lady named Erskine
Who had a remarkable fair skin.
    When I said to her, "Mabel,
    You'd look well in sable."
She answered, "I'm best in my bearskin."

There was an old fellow from Croydon,
Whose cook was a cute little hoyden.
    She would sit on his knees
    While shelling the peas
Or pleasanter duties employed on.

Rebecca, a silly young wench,
Went out on the Thames to catch tench,
     When the boat was upset
     She exclaimed, I regret,
A five-letter word—and in French!

There was a young lady of Eton,
Whose figure had plenty of meat on.
     She said, "Wed me, Jack,
     And you'll find that my back
Is a nice place to warm your cold feet on."

There was an old maid of Genoa;
I blush when I think what Iowa.
     She's gone to her rest,
     And it's all for the best;
Otherwise I would borrow Samoa.

There was a young lady of Florence,
Who for kissing professed great abhorrence;
    But when she'd been kissed
    And found what she'd missed,
She cried till the tears came in torrents.

An oyster from Kalamazoo
Confessed he was feeling quite blue,
    "For," he said, "as a rule,
    When the weather turns cool,
I invariably get in a stew!"

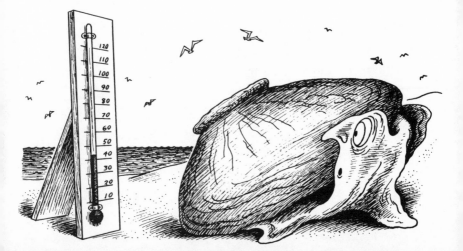

There was a young lady named Rood,
Who was such an absolute prude
    That she pulled down the blind
    When changing her mind
Lest a curious eye should intrude.

There is a young girl of Kilkenny,
Who is worried by lovers so many
    That the saucy young elf
    Means to raffle herself,
And the tickets are two for a penny.

There was a young fellow named Weir,
Who hadn't an atom of fear;
    He indulged a desire
    To touch a live wire . . .
—Most any last line will do here.

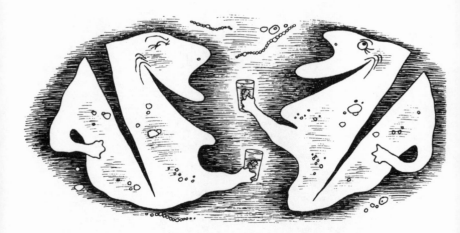

An amoeba named Sam, and his brother,
Were having a drink with each other;
  In the midst of their quaffing
  They split their sides laughing
And each of them now is a mother.

Miss Vera De Peyster Depew
Disdained anything that was new.
  She said, "I do not
  Know exactly What's What
But I know without question Who's Who."

Two beauties who dwelt by the Bosphorus
Had eyes that were brighter than phosphorus.
 The sultan cried "Troth!
 I'll marry you both!"
But they laughed, "I'm afraid you must toss for us."

His mother-in-law's leather lung
Got her young son-in-law so unstrung
 That he pushed her unseen
 In a chopping machine
And canned her and labelled her "Tongue."

There was a young lady of Wilts,
Who walked to the Highland on stilts.
    When they said, "Oh, how shocking,
    To show so much stocking,"
She answered, "Well, what about kilts?"

There was a young lady named Kate,
Who necked in the dark with her date.
    When asked how she fared,
    She said she was scared,
But otherwise doing first-rate.

There once was a lady named Mabel
So ready, so willing, so able,
    And so full of spice
    She could name her own price.
Now Mabel's all wrapped up in sable.

There was a fool gardener of Leeds
Who swallowed six packets of seeds.
    In a month the poor ass
    Was all covered with grass
And he could not sit down for the weeds.

On Matilda's white bosom there leaned
The cheek of a low-minded fiend,
    But she yanked up his head
    And sarcastically said,
"My boy! Won't you *ever* be weaned?"

There was a young girl named Anheuser
Who said that no man could surprise her.
    But Old Overholt
    Gave her virtue a jolt,
And now she is sadder Budweiser.

There was a young lady named Banker,
Who slept while her ship lay at anchor.
    She awoke in dismay
    When she heard the mate say:
"Hi! Hoist up the top-sheet and spanker!"

There was a young fellow of Lyme
Who lived with three wives at a time.
    When asked, "Why the *third?*"
    He said, "One's absurd,
And bigamy, sir, is a crime."

There once was a maid with such graces,
That her curves cried aloud for embraces.
    "You look," cried each he,
    "Like a million to me—
Invested in all the right places!"

There was a young man from the city,
Who saw what he thought was a kitty.
    To make sure of that
    He gave it a pat.
They buried his clothes—what a pity!

There was a fat lady of Clyde
Whose shoelaces once came untied;
    She feared that to bend
    Would display her rear end,
So she cried and she cried and she cried.

There's a notable family named Stein:
There's Gertrude, there's Ep, and there's Ein.
    Gert's prose is the bunk;
    Ep's sculpture is junk;
And no one can understand Ein!

There was a young woman named Riley
Who valued old candle-ends highly;
    When no one was looking
    She used them for cooking.
"It's wicked to waste," she said dryly.

A daring young lady of Guam
Observed, "The Pacific's so calm
    I'll swim out for a lark."
    She met a large shark. . . .
Let us now sing the Ninetieth Psalm.

An important young man from Quebec
Had to welcome the Duchess of Teck.
    So he bought for a dollar
    A very high collar
To save himself washing his neck.

There was an old widower, Doyle,
Who wrapped up his wife in tin foil.
    He thought it would please her
    To stay in the freezer—
And, anyway, outside she'd spoil.

There was a fat man from Lahore,
The same shape behind as before.
    They did not know where
    To offer a chair,
So he had to sit down on the floor.

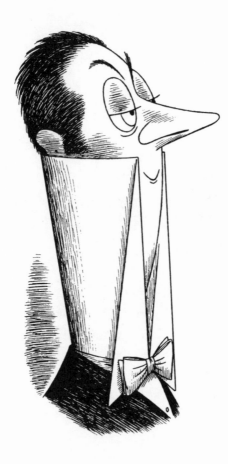

A bather whose clothing was strewed
By winds that had left her quite nude,
    Saw a man come along . . .
    And unless we are wrong,
You thought the next line would be lewd.

There was a young fellow named Sistall
Who shot three old maids with a pistol.
    When 'twas known what he'd done,
    He was given a gun
By the unmarried curates of Bristol.

TRICKS AND PUZZLES

As the limerick grew in favor it also grew in complexity. Its pristine simplicity seemed to be a challenge to make it more sophisticated. Hidden puns became more elaborate; peculiarities in typography offered a fresh field for the trickster. The inconsistencies in spelling and pronunciation were seized upon and exploited to the limit of confusion. To get the full benefit of the following puzzlers the unwary American has to know that in England Beauchamp is pronounced "Beecham," Wemyss is "Weems," Magdalen (when it's Magdalen College) is "Maudlin," Drogheda rhymes with "annoyed her," Sydenham is paired with "hidden 'em," Cholmondeley is always "chumly," Hampshire is familiarly called "Hants," and Salisbury used to be known as "Sarum."

Said a man to his wife down in Sydenham,
"My trousers—where have you hydenham?
    It's perfectly true
    They aren't brand new,
But I foolishly left half-a-quidenham."

A beauty, a perfect divinity,
Till twenty retained her virginity.
    The boys up at Magdalen
    Must have been dawdlin';
It couldn't have happened at Trinity.

There was a young lady named Wemyss
Who, it semyss, was afflicted with dremyss.
    She would wake in the night
    And, in terrible fright,
Shake the bemyss of the house with her scremyss.

A young Irish servant in Drogheda
Had a mistress who often annogheda,
    Whereupon she would swear
    In a language so rare
That thereafter nobody emplogheda.

There was once a maiden named Cholmondeley,
Who every one said was quite colmondeley,
    Yet the maid was so shy,
    That when strangers were ny,
She always would stand around dolmondeley.

There was a young curate of Salisbury
Whose manners were quite halisbury-scalisbury.
    He would wander round Hampshire
    Without any pampshire,
Till the Vicar compelled him to walisbury.

Other puzzlers depend on the eccentricities of irrelevant consonants—Cologne obviously rhymes with "moan"—or abbreviations (oz. for "ounce") or repetitions, or verbal difficulties. Here are some of them.

She frowned and called him Mr.
Because in sport he kr.
    And so in spite
    That very nite
This Mr. kr. sr.

A girl who weighed many an oz.
Used language I dare not pronoz.
    For a fellow unkind
    Pulled her chair out behind
Just to see (so he said) if she'd boz.

When you think of the hosts without No.
Who are slain by the deadly cuco.,
    It's quite a mistake
    Of such food to partake:
It results in a permanent slo.

The sermon our Pastor Rt. Rev.
Began, may have had a rt. clev.,
    But his talk, though consistent,
    Kept the end so far distant
That we left since we felt he mt. nev.

A fly and a flea in a flue
Were imprisoned, so what could they do?
    Said the fly, "Let us flee!"
    "Let us fly!" said the flea.
So they flew through a flaw in the flue.

A bottle of perfume that Willie sent
Was highly displeasing to Millicent.
    Her thanks were so cold
    That they quarreled, I'm told,
Through that silly scent Willie sent Millicent.

There was a young fellow named Fisher,
Who was fishing for fish in a fissure,
     When a cod with a grin
     Pulled the fisherman in . . .
Now they're fishing the fissure for Fisher.

A certain young chap named Bill Beebee
Was in love with a lady named Phoebe.
     "But," said he, "I must see
     What the clerical fee
Be before Phoebe be Phoebe B. Beebee."

There was a young lady from Woosester
Who ussessed to crow like a roosester.
     She ussessed to climb
     Seven trees at a time—
But her sisister ussessed to boosester.

There was a young girl in the choir
Whose voice rose hoir and hoir,
    Till it reached such a height
    It was clear out of seight,
And they found it next day in the spoir.

There once was a bonnie Scotch laddie,
Who said as he put on his plaidie:
    "I've just had a dish
    O' unco' guid fish."
What had he had? had he had haddie?

There's a girl out in Ann Arbor, Mich.,
To meet whom I never would wich.,
    She'd gobble ice cream
    Till with colic she'd scream,
Then order another big dich.

There was a young lady of Lancashire,
Who once went to work as a bank cashier,
But she scarcely knew
$1 + 1 = 2$
So they had to revert to a man cashier.

A rare old bird is the pelican,
His beak holds more than his belican.
He can take in his beak
Enough food for a week.
I'm damned if I know how the helican!

There was a young lady of Twickenham,
Whose boots were too tight to walk quickenham.
She wore them in style,
But after a while
She pulled them both off and was sickenham.

An unpopular youth of Cologne
With a pain in his stomach did mogne.
    He heaved a great sigh
    And said, "I would digh,
But the loss would be only my ogne."

An old couple living in Gloucester
Had a beautiful girl, but they loucester.
    She fell from a yacht,
    And never the spacht
Could be found where the cold waves had toucester.

A boy who played tunes on a comb,
Had become such a nuisance at homb,
    His ma spanked him, and then—
    "Will you do it again?"
And he cheerfully answered her, "Nomb."

There was a young lady of Munich,
Whose appetite simply was unich.
    She contentedly cooed,
     "There's nothing like food,"
As she let out a tuck in her tunich.

The principal food of the Siouxs
Is Indian maize, which they briouxs.
    And then, failing that,
     They'll eat any old hat,
A glove, or a pair of old shiouxs.

There once was a choleric colonel,
Whose oaths were obscene and infolonel,
    And the Chaplain, aghast,
    Gave up protest at last,
But wrote them all down in his jolonel.

A fellow who lived in New Guinea,
Was known as a silly young nuinea.
    He utterly lacked
    Good judgment and tacked,
For he told a plump girl she was skuinea.

Some day ere she grows too antique
My girl's hand in marriage I'll sicque;
    If she's not a coquette
    (Which I'd greatly regruette)
She shall share my ten dollars a wicque.

A bright little maid in St. Thomas
Discovered a suit of pajhomas.
 Said the maiden, "Well, well!
 Whose they are I can't tell.
But I'm sure that those garments St. Mhomas."

Evangeline Alice Du Bois
Committed a dreadful faux pas.
    She loosened a stay
    In her décolleté,
Exposing her je ne sais quoi.

121

There were two young ladies of Birmingham.
I know a sad story concerningham.
　　They stuck needles and pins
　　In the right reverend shins
Of the Bishop engaged in confirmingham.

A globe-trotting man from St. Paul
Made a trip to Japan in the faul.
　　One thing he found out,
　　As he rambled about,
Was that Japanese ladies St. Taul.

A lady there was of Antigua
Who remarked to her spouse, "What a pigua!"
　　He retorted, "My queen,
　　Is it manners you mean,
Or do you refer to my figua?"

A lady, an expert on skis,
Went out with a man who said, "Plis,
On the next precipice
Will you give me a kice?"
She said, "Quick! Before somebody sis!"

Said a lively young nurse out in Padua
To her master, "Please, sir, you're a dadua.
I've come for some pins
For to wrap up the twins,
And to hear you remark, sir, how gladua."

There was a young poet of Trinity
Who, although he could trill like a linnet, he
Could never complete
Any poem with feet,
Saying, "Idiots,
Can't you see
that what I'm writing
happens
to be
Free
Verse?"

125

An adroit versifier and expert compiler, Carolyn Wells made a specialty of tongue-twisters and "Anglicisms." Her carefully manipulated syllables resulted in conclusions that were both logical and grotesque. For example:

Said a bad little youngster named Beauchamp:
"Those jelly tarts, how shall I reauchamp?
    To my parents I'd go
    But they always say 'No,'
No matter how much I beseauchamp."

A tutor who tooted the flute
Tried to tutor two tooters to toot.
    Said the two to the tutor,
    "Is it harder to toot, or
To tutor two tooters to toot?"

A very polite man named Hawarden
Went out to plant flowers in his gawarden.
    If he trod on a slug,
    A worm or a bug,
He would instantly say, "I beg pawarden."

There was a young fellow named Tait,
Who dined with his girl at 8:08.
    But I'd hate to relate
    What that fellow named Tait
And his tête-à-tête ate at 8:08!

A canner, exceedingly canny,
One morning remarked to his granny:
    "A canner can can
    Anything that he can,
But a canner can't can a can, can he?"

Today's young scientists have used limericks to force physical laws to tricky and puzzling conclusions. To these purists the limerick must be logically true to the textbook. The following examples carry Einstein's theory of relativity to the height of the ridiculous.

A rocket explorer named Wright
Once traveled much faster than light.
    He set out one day
    In a relative way,
And returned on the previous night.

A fencing instructor named Fisk
In duels was terribly brisk.
    So fast was his action,
    The Fitzgerald contraction
Foreshortened his foil to a disk.

SIMPLY RIDICULOUS

The original limericks were founded on nonsense; they revolved around nonsensical ideas, places, and situations. The modern limerick writers follow in the footsteps of their predecessors. They too push queerness to and even beyond the point of absurdity and often abandon meaning altogether. A few attempt to make sense, but most of them stick to the traditional wild thoughts and crazy conceptions. There are those who maintain that the best limericks are those which are not merely simple but simply ridiculous.

There was an old man of Peru
Who dreamt he was eating a shoe.
    He awoke in the night
    With a terrible fright
And found it was perfectly true!

There was an old man of Boolong
Who frightened the birds with his song.
    It wasn't the words
    Which astonished the birds
But the horrible *dooble ontong*.

There was a young girl from Asturias
Whose temper was frantic and furious.
    She used to throw eggs
    At her grandmother's legs—
A habit unpleasant but curious.

We thought him an absolute lamb;
But when he sat down in the jam
    On taking his seat
    At our Sunday School treat,
We all heard the Vicar say "——!
  —er—stand up please while I say grace."

There was an odd fellow of Tyre,
Who constantly sat on the fire.
   When asked, "Are you hot?"
   He said, "Certainly not.
I'm James Winterbotham, Esquire."

There was a young lady who tried
A diet of apples, and died.
   The unfortunate miss
   Really perished of this:
Too much cider inside her inside.

There was a young lady of Tottenham,
Her manners—she'd wholly forgotten 'em.
    While at tea at the Vicar's,
    She took off her knickers,
Explaining she felt much too hot in 'em.

There was a queer lady named Harris,
Whom nothing could ever embarrass
    Till the bath salts she shook
    In the bath that she took
Turned out to be plaster of Paris.

There was a young curate of Minster
Who admonished a giddy young spinster.
    For she used, on the ice,
    Words not at all nice
When he, at a turn, slid against her.

There was a young parson named Perkins
Exceedingly fond of small gherkins.
    One summer at tea
    He ate forty-three,
Which pickled his internal workins.

There was a kind curate of Kew,
Who kept a large cat in a pew;
    There he taught it each week
    A new letter of Greek,
But it never got further than *Mu*.

There was an old codger of Broome,
Who kept a baboon in his room.
  "It reminds me," he said,
  "Of a friend who is dead."
But he never would tell us of whom.

There was an old lady of Harrow
Whose views were exceedingly narrow.
    At the end of her paths
    She built two bird baths
For the different sexes of sparrow.

There was a young fellow named Sydney,
Who drank till he ruined his kidney.
    It shriveled and shrank,
    As he sat there and drank,
But he'd had a good time at it, didn' he?

There were three little birds in a wood,
Who always sang hymns when they could;
    What the words were about
    They could never make out,
But they felt it was doing them good.

A cheese that was aged and gray
Was walking and talking one day.
    Said the cheese, "Kindly note
    My mama was a goat
And I'm made out of curds by the whey."

There was a young lady of York
Who was shortly expecting the stork,
When the doctor walked in
With a businesslike grin,
A pickax, a spade, and a fork.

There was a young man of Bengal
Who went to a fancy-dress ball,
    He went, just for fun,
    Dressed up as a bun,
And a dog ate him up in the hall.

There was a young maid of Ostend,
Who swore she'd hold out to the end;
  But alas! half-way over,
  'Twixt Calais and Dover,
She done what she didn't intend.

A barber who lived in Batavia,
Was known for his fearless behavia.
  An enormous baboon
  Broke in his saloon,
But he murmured, "I'm damned if I'll shavia."

There was a young lady of Lynn,
Who was so uncommonly thin
  That when she essayed
  To drink lemonade,
She slipped through the straw and fell in.

There was an old lady of Rye,
Who was baked by mistake in a pie,
    To the household's disgust
    She emerged through the crust,
And exclaimed, with a yawn, "Where am I?"

A cannibal bold of Penzance
Ate an uncle and two of his aunts,
    A cow and her calf,
    An ox and a half—
And now he can't button his pants.

An eccentric old person of Slough,
Who took all his meals with a cow,
    Always said, "It's uncanny,
    She's so like Aunt Fanny,"
But he never would indicate how.

There was an old lady of Brooking,
Who had a great genius for cooking;
    She could bake sixty pies
    All quite the same size,
And tell which was which without looking.

There was a young maid who said, "Why
Can't I look in my ear with my eye?
    If I give my mind to it,
    I'm sure I can do it;
You never can tell till you try."

There was an old man of Calcutta
Who spoke with a terrible stutter.
    At breakfast he said,
    "Give me b-b-b-bread,
And b-b-b-b-b-b-butter."

A dancing-girl came from St. Gall
With a mouth so exceedingly small,
    That she said, "It would be
    Much more easy for me
To do without eating at all!"

150

There was an old lady of Herm,
Who tied bows on the tail of a worm;
    Said she, "You look festive,
    But don't become restive,
You'll wriggle 'em off if you squirm."

There was an old man of Blackheath,
Who sat on his set of false teeth;
    Said he, with a start,
      "O Lord, bless my heart!
I've bitten myself underneath!"

A classical scholar from Flint
Developed a curious squint.
    With her left-handed eye
    She could scan the whole sky
While the other was reading small print.

There was an old lady of Kent
Whose nose was remarkably bent.
    One day, they suppose,
    She followed her nose,
For no one knows which way she went.

The village was giddy with rumors
Of a goat who was suffering from tumors.
        Cans and library paste
        Were quite to his taste,
But he choked on Elizabeth's bloomers.

The mouth of a glutton named Moto
Was the size that no organ should grow to.
        It could take in with ease
        Six carrots, ten peas,
And a whole baked potato in toto.

There was an old skinflint named Green,
Who grew so abnormally lean
        And flat and compressed,
        That his back squeezed his chest,
And sideways he couldn't be seen.

An odd-looking girl from Devizes
Had eyes of two different sizes.
>   The one was so small
>   It was nothing at all;
But the other took several prizes.

There was a young lady from Lynn
Who was sunk in original sin.
>   When they said, "Do be good,"
>   She replied, "If I could . . .
But I'd *do* wrong right over ag'in."

As they fished his old plane from the sea
The inventor just chortled with glee.
>   "I shall build," and he laughed,
>   "A submarine craft,
And perhaps it will fly. We shall see."

There was a young man of Japan,
Who wrote verse that never would scan.
    When they said, "But the thing
    Doesn't go with a swing,"
He said, "Yes, but I always like to get as many
    words into the last line as I possibly *can*."

In Paris some visitors go
To see what no person should know.
    And then there are tourists,
    The purest of purists,
Who say it is quite *comme il faut*.

There was a strange creature named Marks
Whose idea of diversions and larks
    Was stirring up tramps,
    Disturbing boys' camps,
And defacing nude statues in parks.

Said Oedipus Rex, growing red,
"Those head-shrinkers! Would they were dead!
    They make such a pother
    Because I love mother.
Well, should I love father instead!"

J. A. LEVENTHAL

LIGHTLY AMATORY

This, as the title indicates, shows what the limerick makers have done with the perennial theme of Love. It would be too much to expect love songs and lyrics in the traditional manner, and those who are seeking anything of this nature should look elsewhere. The five-line examples are light-minded and not to be taken at all seriously. They are, however, pleasing and provocative in their very casualness; they are nimble, a little naughty, sometimes bold but never really brazen.

Said a pretty young student named Smith,
Whose virtue was largely a myth,
    "Try hard as I can
    I can't find a man
Who it's fun to be virtuous with."

You have written a sonnet, said Chloe,
On my bosom so rounded and snowy.
    You have sent me some verse on
    Each part of my person.
That's lovely. Now *do* something, bo-y!

A cautious young girl from Penzance
Decided to take just one chance.
    She wavered, then lo,
    She let herself go . . .
Now all of her sisters are aunts.

A sculptor remarked, "I'm afraid
I've fallen in love with my trade.
    I'm much too elated
    With what I've created
And, chiefly, the women I've made."

The classical sculptor called Phidias
Whose knowledge of art was insidious,
    Once carved Aphrodite
    Without any nightie,
Which shocked all the purely fastidious.

A young country boy from Pitlochery
Kissed a much made-up girl in a rockery.
    When he tasted the paint
    He cried, "Lassie, this ain't
A real kiss at all. It's a mockery."

There was a fierce soldier from Parma,
Who lovingly fondled his charmer.
    Said the maiden demure,
    "It's delightful, I'm sure,
But it's better without all that armor."

167

A strip-teaser up in Fall River
Caused a sensitive fellow to quiver.
    The esthetic vibration
    Brought soulful elation.
Besides, it was good for his liver.

There was a young charmer named Sheba
Whose pet was a darling amoeba.
    This queer blob of jelly
    Would lie on her belly,
And blissfully murmur, *"Ich liebe."*

When her daughter got married in Whister
Her mother remarked as she kissed her,
    "That fellow you've won
    Is sure to be fun—
Since tea he's kissed me and your sister."

There was a young poet of Thusis,
Who took twilight walks with the Muses.
　　But these nymphs of the air
　　Are not quite what they were,
And the practice has led to abuses.

A young girl from old Aberystwyth
Brought grain to the mill to get grist with.
　　But the miller's son Jack
　　Sighed, "A lass and a lack,"
And united the things that they kissed with.

"Austerity now is the fashion,"
Remarked a young lady with passion.
　　Then she glanced at the bed,
　　And quietly said,
"There's one thing no nation can ration."

As Mozart composed a sonata
The maid bent to fasten her garter.
 There was no delaying;
 He started in playing
Un poco piu appassionata.

There was a young maiden of Siam
Who said to her lover, young Kiam,
     "If you kiss me, of course
     You will have to use force—
But God knows you are stronger than I am."

There was a young person named May
Who never let men have their way.
     But a brawny young spark
     One night in the park . . .
Now she goes to the park every day.

There was a young writer named Smith,
Whose virtue was largely a myth.
     We knew that he did it;
     He couldn't have hid it—
The question was only who with.

A much-worried mother once said,
"My dear, you've been kissing young Fred
    Since six; it's now ten.
    Do it just once again,
And then think of going to bed."

A girl who would not be disgraced
Would flee from all lovers in haste.
    It all went quite well
    Till one day she fell . . .
She sometimes still dreams that she's chaste.

A free-living damsel named Hall
Once went to a birth control ball.
    She took an appliance
    To make love with science;
But nobody asked her at all.

There once was a lady from Nantes
Très chic and très élégante
    But her mouth was so small
    It was no use at all
Except for la plume de ma tante.

There was a young girl from Detroit
Who at kissing was very adroit;
    She could pucker her lips
    Into total eclipse,
Or open them out like a quoit.

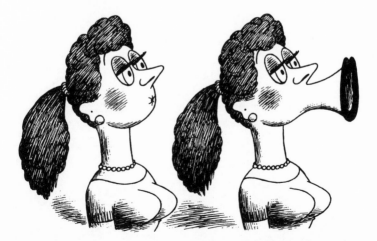

ROLLICKING AND ROWDY

It has been said that there are three kinds of limericks: limericks that can be told to ladies, limericks that can be repeated to clergymen—and limericks. Arnold Bennett put it more succinctly: he maintained that the only good limericks were either reprehensible or just unprintable. The latter are unquestionably the most popular although not the most readily obtainable. Nevertheless, they have been cherished by all sorts of people, respected statesmen as well as social outcasts, even by Puritans to whom most things are impure.

This concluding section includes slightly paraphrased versions of what many have considered (in their original forms) unprintable though not unspeakable. With the alteration of a word or two, they have been heard at countless cocktail parties and other occasions where Good Fellows (and their feminine counterparts) Get Together. It is recommended that they be taken in small sips rather than large gulps. In that way they will serve as a refreshing and effervescent if somewhat highly flavored tonic . . . with or without gin.

When the First Selectman took advantage
Of a lovely young lady of Wantage,
    The County Surveyor
    Said, "You'll have to pay her,
For you've altered the line of her frontage."

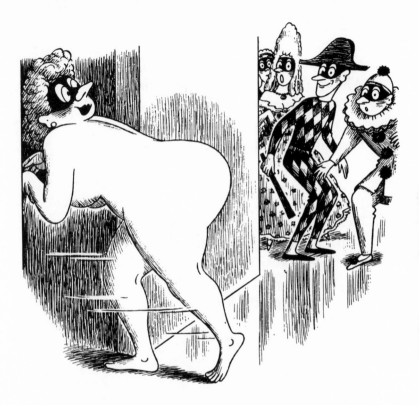

A corpulent maiden named Kroll,
Had a notion exceedingly droll:
    At a masquerade ball,
    Dressed in nothing at all,
She backed in as a Parker House roll.

There was a young lady of Kent
Who said that she knew what it meant
    When men asked her to dine
    Upon lobster and wine.
She knew. Oh, she knew! But she went.

There was an old monk in Siberia
Whose existence grew steadily drearier,
    Till he broke from his cell
    With a hell of a yell
And eloped with the Mother Superior.

There once was a maître d'hôtel
Who said, "They can all go to hell!
    They make love to my wife
    And it ruins my life,
For the worst is, they do it so well!"

There was a young man from Racine
Who invented a funny machine.
    Concave and convex
    It would suit either sex—
The goddamnedest thing ever seen.

Three lovely young girls from St. Thomas
Attended dance-halls in pajamas.
    They were fondled all summer
    By sax, bass, and drummer—
I'm surprised that by now they're not mamas.

There was a young wife who begat
Three husky boys, Nat, Pat, and Tat.
    They all yelled for food,
    And a problem ensued
When she found there was no tit for Tat.

There was a most finicky lass
Who always wore panties of brass.
     When they asked, "Don't they chafe?"
     She said, "Yes, but I'm safe
From pinches and pins in the—grass."

182

There was a young gaucho named Bruno,
Who said, "Love is all that I *do* know.
    A tall girl is fine;
    A short one's divine;
But a llama is Numero Uno!"

A cute debutante from St. Paul
Wore a newspaper dress to a ball.
    The dress caught on fire,
    And burnt her entire
Front page, sporting section, and all.

There was a young student at Johns
Who attempted to fondle the swans.
    Whereupon said the porter,
    "Oh, pray take my daughter.
The birds are reserved for the dons."

The girls who frequent picture-palaces
Have no use for psychoanalysis.
    And though Doctor Freud
    Would be sorely annoyed,
They stick to their old-fashioned fallacies.

There is a sad rumor that Mona
Goes around in a black net kimona.
 Don't think for a minute
 There's anything in it—
Anything much besides Mona.

To his bride said the lynx-eyed detective,
"Can it be that my eyesight's defective?
 Has your east tit the least bit
 The best of the west tit?
Or is it a trick of perspective?"

There is a young blue blood named Maude,
A frightful society fraud.
 In company she
 Is as cold as could be,
But get her alone—O my Gawd!

186

There once was a rake known as Baker
Who tried to seduce a fair Quaker.
    And when he had done it,
    She straightened her bonnet,
And said, "I give thanks to my maker."

There was a pert lass from Madras
Who had a remarkable ass—
    Not rounded and pink,
    As you probably think.
It was gray, had long ears, and ate grass.

There was a young lady named Hopper
Who came a society cropper.
    She determined to go
    To Bordeaux with her beau . . .
The rest of the story's improper.

There was a young lady from Thrace
Whose corsets no longer would lace.
    Her mother said, "Nelly,
    There's more in your belly
Than ever went in through your face."

A lissom psychotic named Jane
Once kissed every man on a train;
    Said she: "Please don't panic;
    I'm just nymphomanic—
It wouldn't be fun were I sane."

A handsome young bastard named Ray
Was conceived on the Rue de la Paix.
    According to law,
    He can name you his maw,
But as for his pa, *je ne sais.*

JOHN F. MOORE

Said a calendar model named Gloria,
"So the men can enjoy real euphoria,
    You pose as you are
    In Jan., Feb. and Mar.
Then in April they wanna see moria!"

Have you heard about Madam Lupescu,
Who came to Rumania's rescue?
    It's a wonderful thing
    To be under a king.
Is democracy better? I eskyou!

In the Garden of Eden sat Adam,
Disporting himself with his madam.
    She was filled with elation,
    For in all of creation
There was only one man—and she had'm.